Diabetic Smoothies Recipe Book:

Healthy and Easy Diabetic Diet Cookbook

By

Viktoria McCartney

Copyright [Viktoria McCartney]

Contents

Introduction

Have you ever wondered if you could have a delicious smoothie without worrying about your blood sugar levels? Whether you've been living with diabetes for a while or have just been diagnosed, we all dream of enjoying a tasty treat that doesn't harm your health. Well, you're in luck! Welcome to the world of Diabetic-Friendly Smoothies.

Managing diabetes can feel like an uphill battle; we often must give up our favorite foods and flavors to stay healthy. But what if we told you that you don't have to choose between taste and well-being? This book is your guide to creating smoothies that not only fit within the bounds of your diabetic diet but also tantalize your taste buds.

Permissible & Non-Permissible Ingredients for Diabetic Smoothies

The secret to making diabetic-friendly smoothies lies in understanding which ingredients are safe and which you should avoid. We all know sugar is a big concern, but there's much more to it than that. Our journey through these pages will take you on an exploration of ingredients and their profound impact on your health.

Before we start blending and sipping, let's take a moment to grasp the essence of this book.

Imagine relishing a cool, flavorful smoothie without worrying about how it will affect your blood sugar or sipping on a creamy, fruity concoction that satisfies your cravings and supports your overall health. This is precisely what we aim to accomplish with this book.

The upcoming chapters will unfold the mysteries surrounding diabetes and dietary restrictions. We'll explore the fascinating science behind the condition and how certain ingredients can help or hinder your well-being. Most importantly, we'll equip you with the knowledge and skills to create smoothies that align perfectly with your health goals.

This is more than just another cookbook. It's your passport to a world filled with flavors, colors, and textures that cater to your specific dietary needs. Whether you're a seasoned diabetes veteran or have recently been introduced to this condition, you'll discover valuable insights, delectable recipes, and practical tips to help you navigate the realm of diabetic-friendly smoothies with ease and confidence.

Before we explore the world of ingredients, let's break down the core concepts:

Permissible Ingredients: Your Allies for Good Health

Creating diabetic-friendly smoothies centres around choosing the right ingredients. You'll soon learn that there's an abundance of options that enhance the taste and texture and offer substantial health benefits. Fresh fruits, vegetables, nuts, and seeds will become your trusted companions on this journey. In the pages ahead, we'll delve into these ingredients, highlighting their nutritional value and explaining how they can seamlessly integrate into your daily meal plan.

If you're concerned about satisfying your sweet tooth, rest assured that nature has a solution. We'll introduce you to natural sweeteners like stevia, monk fruit, and Erythritol, which provide sweetness without sending your blood sugar on a rollercoaster ride.

We'll explore a variety of fiber-rich ingredients that play a pivotal role in stabilizing your blood sugar levels. From oats and chia seeds to flaxseed meal and psyllium husk, these elements contribute thickness and body to your smoothies and facilitate a gradual release of energy throughout the day.

Non-Permissible Ingredients: The Culprits to Avoid

Now, let's talk about the ingredients that should have no place in your diabetic-friendly smoothies. Sugar, in all its forms, tops the list of offenders. However, it's essential to recognize that some seemingly healthy ingredients can also threaten your blood sugar control. We'll expose these hidden culprits that often sneak into smoothies, jeopardizing your health.

Artificial sweeteners may appear to be a safe choice, but we'll demystify their potential impact on your body and help you make informed decisions. We'll also shed light on common pitfalls like high-carb fruits and fruit juices, which can send your blood sugar levels soaring.

Our intention is not to overwhelm you with rules but to empower you with knowledge. By understanding which ingredients to steer clear of and why, you'll be better equipped to make informed choices and adapt recipes to suit your unique requirements.

The Trend of Smoothies

In recent years, smoothies have become more than just a drink; they've become a lifestyle. The trend of sipping on these vibrant concoctions has swept across the globe. You've probably seen smoothie shops popping up on every street corner, offering an array of colorful blends with catchy names.

What's driving this trend? Part of it is our craving for health. In a world where we're constantly on the move, smoothies offer a convenient and nutritious solution. They're not just for breakfast; they can replace any meal. Whether rushing to work, running errands, or heading to the gym, a well-crafted smoothie can be your trusty companion.

Smoothies provide a way to pack various nutrients into a single glass. They offer a quick and easy method to meet your dietary goals while satisfying your taste buds. Plus, they're versatile. You can tailor your smoothie to match your cravings and nutritional requirements.

Amid our busy lives, the convenience of sipping a meal in a portable cup is undeniably appealing. It's a trend here to stay because it aligns with our desire to lead healthier lives without sacrificing flavor.

So, are you ready to begin this delectable and healthful adventure? Get set to blend, sip, and enjoy better health. It's a voyage into the heart of flavor, nutrition, and well-being, where the world of smoothies becomes a canvas for your creativity, and diabetes management becomes a seamless part of your vibrant and fulfilling life. Over the following pages, we'll provide the tools, tips, and mouthwatering recipes to make your diabetic journey a truly delightful one. Let's commence your path to better health, one sip at a time.

Strawberry Smoothie

Prep time: 10 minutes ∣Serves: 2 ∣ Per Serving: Calories 80, Carbs 17.8g,
Fat 0.8g, Protein 2.3g

Ingredients:

- Fresh strawberries – 2 C.
- Chilled coconut water – 1½ C.
- Ice cubes – ¼ C.

Directions:

1) Put strawberries and remnant ingredients into a high-power
   blender and process to form a smooth and creamy smoothie.
2) Enjoy immediately.

Strawberry Yogurt Smoothie

Prep time: 10 minutes | Serves: 2 | Per Serving: Calories 80, Carbs 13.3g, Fat 2.1g, Protein 3.8g

Ingredients:

- Fresh strawberries – 1½ C.
- Fat-free plain yogurt – ½ C.
- Unsweetened almond milk – 1 C.
- Ice cubes – ¼ C.

Directions:

1) Put strawberries and remnant ingredients into a high-power blender and process to form a smooth and creamy smoothie.
2) Enjoy immediately.

Strawberry Almond Smoothie

Prep time: 10 minutes |Serves: 2 | Per Serving: Calories 133, Carbs 12.4g,
Fat 8.9g, Protein 4g

Ingredients:

- Frozen strawberries – 1½ C.
- Almonds – ¼ C. cut up
- Liquid stevia – 3-4 drops
- Unsweetened almond milk – 1½ C.

Directions:

1) Put strawberries and remnant ingredients into a high-power blender and process to form a smooth and creamy smoothie.
2) Enjoy immediately.

Strawberry & Rhubarb Smoothie

Prep time: 10 minutes | Serves: 2 | Per Serving: Calories 105, Carbs 16.7g, Fat 3.1g, Protein 4.6g

Ingredients:

- Rhubarb – 1 C., cut up
- Frozen strawberries – 1½ C.
- Vanilla extract – ½ tsp.
- Fat-free Plain Yogurt – ½ C.
- Unsweetened almond milk – 1½ C.
- Ice cubes – ¼ C.

Directions:

1) Put rhubarb and remnant ingredients into a high-power blender and process to form a smooth and creamy smoothie.
2) Enjoy immediately.

Strawberry & Plum Smoothie

Prep time: 10 minutes |Serves: 2 | Per Serving: Calories 100, Carbs 24g, Fat 1g, Protein 0.5g

Ingredients:

- Frozen strawberries – 2 C.
- Medium-sized plum – 1, pitted and cut up
- Green Tea – 1 C. brewed and cooled
- Unsweetened almond milk – ½ C.
- Ice cubes – ¼ C.

Directions:

1) Put strawberries and remnant ingredients into a high-power blender and process to form a smooth and creamy smoothie.
2) Enjoy immediately.

Raspberry, Cabbage & Tomato Smoothie

Prep time: 10 minutes | Serves: 2 | Per Serving: Calories 70, Carbs 16.9g, Fat 0.5g, Protein 1.6g

Ingredients:

- Fresh raspberries – 1 C.
- Red cabbage – 1 C. cut up
- Small-sized tomato – 1, cut up
- Liquid stevia – 3-4 drops
- Filtered water – 1½ C.
- Ice cubes – ¼ C.

Directions:

1) Put raspberries and remnant ingredients into a high-power blender and process to form a smooth and creamy smoothie.
2) Enjoy immediately.

Blackberry Smoothie

Prep time: 10 minutes | Serves: 2 | Per Serving: Calories 136, Carbs 26.4g, Fat 0.8g, Protein 6.4g

Ingredients:

- Fresh blackberries – 2 C.
- Vanilla extract – ¼ tsp.
- Fresh orange juice – ½ C.
- Fat-free milk – 1 C.
- Ice cubes – ¼ C.

Directions:

1) Put blackberries and remnant ingredients into a high-power blender and process to form a smooth and creamy smoothie.
2) Enjoy immediately.

Blackberry & Spinach Smoothie

Prep time: 10 minutes |Serves: 2 | Per Serving: Calories 90, Carbs 10g, Fat 4.8g, Protein 3.9g

Ingredients:

- Fresh spinach – 2 C.
- Frozen blackberries – 1 C.
- Hemp seeds – 1 tbsp.
- Fresh lemon juice – 1 tsp.
- Unsweetened almond milk – 1½ C.
- Ice cubes – ¼ C.

Directions:

1) Put spinach and remnant ingredients into a high-power blender and process to form a smooth and creamy smoothie.
2) Enjoy immediately.

Blueberry Smoothie

Prep time: 10 minutes | Serves: 2 | Per Serving: Calories 128, Carbs 27g,
Fat 0.5g, Protein 5.1g

Ingredients:

- Fresh blueberries – 2 C.
- Fat-free milk – 1 C.
- Ice cubes – ¼ C.

Directions:

1) Put blueberries and remnant ingredients into a high-power blender and process to form a smooth and creamy smoothie.
2) Enjoy immediately.

Blueberry & Spinach Smoothie

Prep time: 10 minutes |Serves: 2 | Per Serving: Calories 74, Carbs 10.8g, Fat 3.3g, Protein 2.2g

Ingredients:

- Fresh blueberries – 1 C.
- Fresh spinach – 2 C.
- Flaxseeds meal – 1 tsp.
- Liquid stevia – 3-4 drops
- Unsweetened almond milk – 1½ C.
- Ice cubes – ¼ C.

Directions:

1) Put blueberries and remnant ingredients into a high-power blender and process to form a smooth and creamy smoothie.
2) Enjoy immediately.

Berries & Orange Smoothie

Prep time: 10 minutes | Serves: 2 | Per Serving: Calories 153, Carbs 31.6g,
Fat 0.5g, Protein 6.7g

Ingredients:

- Large-sized orange – 1, peeled, seeded and sectioned
- Fresh mixed berries – 1½ C.
- Fat-free plain yogurt – 1 C.
- Ice cubes – ½ C.

Directions:

1) Put orange pieces and remnant ingredients into a high-power blender and process to form a smooth and creamy smoothie.
2) Enjoy immediately.

Berries & Avocado Smoothie

Prep time: 10 minutes |Serves: 2 | Per Serving: Calories 181, Carbs 9.5g,
Fat 16.1g, Protein 2.3g

Ingredients:

- Frozen blueberries – ½ C.
- Frozen strawberries – ½ C.
- Medium-sized avocado – ½, peeled, pitted and sliced
- Flaxseeds – 1 tsp.
- Fat-free plain yogurt – 6 ounces
- Unsweetened almond milk – 1 C.
- Ice cubes – ¼ C.

Directions:

1) Put blueberries and remnant ingredients into a high-power blender and process to form a smooth and creamy smoothie.
2) Enjoy immediately.

Berries, Spinach & Celery Smoothie

Prep time: 10 minutes │Serves: 2 │ Per Serving: Calories 117, Carbs 11.6g,
Fat 1.1g, Protein 14.8g

Ingredients:

- Frozen mixed berries – 1 C.
- Fresh spinach – 3 C.
- Celery stalk – 1 C. cut up
- Fresh ginger 1 (2-inch) piece, peeled and cut up
- Unsweetened protein powder – 1 scoop
- Filtered water – 1½ C.
- Ice cubes – ¼ C.

Directions:

1) Put berries and remnant ingredients into a high-power blender and process to form a smooth and creamy smoothie.
2) Enjoy immediately.

Orange, Strawberry & Spinach Smoothie

Prep time: 10 minutes │Serves: 2 │ Per Serving: Calories 134, Carbs 23.8g, Fat 0.4g, Protein 9.3g

Ingredients:

- Small-sized orange – 1, peeled, seeded and sectioned
- Fresh strawberries – 1 C. hulled and sliced
- Fresh spinach – 2 C.
- Fat-free Plain Yogurt – ½ C.
- Fat-free milk – 1¼ C.
- Ice cubes – ¼ C.

Directions:

1) Put orange and remnant ingredients into a high-power blender and process to form a smooth and creamy smoothie.
2) Enjoy immediately.

Peach & Juices Smoothie

Prep time: 10 minutes | Serves: 2 | Per Serving: Calories 184, Carbs 36.2g, Fat 3g, Protein 4.3g

Ingredients:

- Frozen peach slices – 2 C.
- Flaxseed meal – 2 tbsp.
- Fresh ginger – 1 tbsp. cut up
- Fresh orange juice – 1 C.
- Fresh carrot juice – 1 C.

Directions:

1) Put peach slices and remnant ingredients into a high-power blender and process to form a smooth and creamy smoothie.
2) Enjoy immediately.

Peach & Yogurt Smoothie

Prep time: 10 minutes │Serves: 2 │ Per Serving: Calories 84, Carbs 15.9g,
Fat 0.4g, Protein 4.8g

Ingredients:

- Fresh peaches – 1½ C. sliced
- Fat-free plain yogurt – ¼ C.
- Liquid stevia 3-4 drops –
- Skim milk – ½ C.
- Ice cubes – 1 C.

Directions:

1) Put peach slices and remnant ingredients into a high-power blender and process to form a smooth and creamy smoothie.
2) Enjoy immediately.

Spiced Peach Smoothie

Prep time: 10 minutes | Serves: 2 | Per Serving: Calories 101, Carbs 17.5g, Fat 3.6g, Protein 2.6g

Ingredients:

- Frozen peach slices – 2 C.
- Chia seeds – 1 tsp.
- Ground ginger – ½ tsp.
- Ground cinnamon – ½ tsp.
- Liquid stevia – 3-4 drops
- Unsweetened almond milk – 1½ C.

Directions:

1) Put peach pieces and remnant ingredients into a high-power blender and process to form a smooth and creamy smoothie.
2) Enjoy immediately.

Peach & Apricots Smoothie

Prep time: 10 minutes ǀ Serves: 2 ǀ Per Serving: Calories 114, Carbs 20.9g, Fat 3.5g, Protein 20.9g

Ingredients:

- Peach – 1¼ C. peeled, pitted, and cut up
- Apricots – 1¼ C. pitted and cut up
- Unsweetened almond milk – 1½ C.
- Ice cubes – ¼ C.

Directions:

1) Put peach and remnant ingredients into a high-power blender and process to form a smooth and creamy smoothie.
2) Enjoy immediately.

Apricot Yogurt Smoothie

Prep time: 10 minutes | Serves: 2 | Per Serving: Calories 156, Carbs 30.4g,
Fat 0.9g, Protein 9.2g

Ingredients:

- Apricots – 2 C. pitted and cut up
- Fat-free plain yogurt – 1 C.
- Fat-free milk – ½ C.
- Ice cubes – ¼ C.

Directions:

1) Put apricots and remnant ingredients into a high-power blender and process to form a smooth and creamy smoothie.
2) Enjoy immediately.

Apricot, Peach & Carrot Smoothie

Prep time: 10 minutes | Serves: 2 | Per Serving: Calories 105, Carbs 24.7g, Fat 0.9g, Protein 2.6g

Ingredients:

- Apricots – 4, pitted and cut up
- Peaches – 1, pitted and cut up
- Medium-sized Carrot – 1, peeled and cut up
- Filtered water – 1½ C.
- Ice cubes – ¼ C.

Directions:

1) Put apricots and remnant ingredients into a high-power blender and process to form a smooth and creamy smoothie.
2) Enjoy immediately.

Apricot & Apple Smoothie

Prep time: 10 minutes |Serves: 2 | Per Serving: Calories 156, Carbs 39.6g,
Fat 1g, Protein 2.4g

Ingredients:

- Apricots – 4, pitted and cut up
- Medium-sized green apples – 2, peeled, cored and cut up
- Fresh spinach – 2 C.
- Filtered water – 1½ C.
- Ice cubes – ¼ C.

Directions:

1) Put apricots and remnant ingredients into a high-power blender and process to form a smooth and creamy smoothie.
2) Enjoy immediately.

Plums & Avocado Smoothie

Prep time: 10 minutes | Serves: 2 | Per Serving: Calories 183, Carbs 15.5g, Fat 1.4g, Protein 3.2g

Ingredients:

- Large-sized plums – 2, pitted and cut up
- Small-sized avocado – 1, peeled, pitted and cut up
- Fresh spinach – 2 C.
- Unsweetened almond milk – 1½ C.
- Ice cubes – ¼ C.

Directions:

1) Put plums and remnant ingredients into a high-power blender and process to form a smooth and creamy smoothie.
2) Enjoy immediately.

Papaya & Apple Smoothie

Prep time: 10 minutes |Serves: 2 | Per Serving: Calories 123, Carbs 31.7g,
Fat 0.7g, Protein 1.1g

Ingredients:

- Filtered water – 1½ C.
- Papaya – 2 C peeled and cut up
- Large-sized apple – 1, peeled, cored, and cut up
- Fresh ginger – 1 tsp. peeled and cut up
- Ice cubes – ¼ C.

Directions:

1) Put papaya and remnant ingredients into a high-power blender and process to form a smooth and creamy smoothie.
2) Enjoy immediately.

Apple & Almonds Smoothie

Prep time: 10 minutes | Serves: 2 | Per Serving: Calories 221, Carbs 39.4g, Fat 6.3g, Protein 7.1g

Ingredients:

- Large-sized apples – 2, peeled, cored and sliced
- Almonds – 4 tbsp., cut up
- Vanilla extract – ¼ tsp.
- Fat-free milk – 1 C.
- Ice cubes – ½ C.

Directions:

1) Put apples and remnant ingredients into a high-power blender and process to form a smooth and creamy smoothie.
2) Enjoy immediately.

Apple & Carrot Smoothie

Prep time: 10 minutes │Serves: 2 │ Per Serving: Calories 87, Carbs 21.3g,
Fat 0.4g, Protein 2.1g

Ingredients:

- Large-sized green apple – 1, peeled, cored and cut up
- Carrot – 1, peeled and cut up
- Fresh mustard greens – 2 C. trimmed and cut up
- Fresh lemon juice – 1 tbsp.
- Filtered water – 1½ C.
- Ice cubes – ¼ C.

Directions:

1) Put apple and remnant ingredients into a high-power blender and process to form a smooth and creamy smoothie.
2) Enjoy immediately.

Apple & Kale Smoothie

Prep time: 10 minutes | Serves: 2 | Per Serving: Calories 153, Carbs 38.4g, Fat 0.5g, Protein 2.8g

Ingredients:

- Green apples – 2, peeled, cored and cut up
- Celery stalk – 1, cut up
- Fresh kale – 2 C. trimmed and cut up
- Fresh parsley leaves – 2 tbsp.
- Fresh lemon juice – ½ tbsp.
- Chilled filtered water – 2 C.

Directions:

1) Put apple and remnant ingredients into a high-power blender and process to form a smooth and creamy smoothie.
2) Enjoy immediately.

Apple & Broccoli Smoothie

Prep time: 10 minutes | Serves: 2 | Per Serving: Calories 181, Carbs 21.8g, Fat 11.3g, Protein 2g

Ingredients:

- Large-sized apple – 1 peeled, cored and sliced
- Small-sized avocado – 1, peeled, pitted and cut up
- Broccoli Florets – ½ C. cut up
- Chilled filtered water – 2 C.

Directions:

1) Put apple and remnant ingredients into a high-power blender and process to form a smooth and creamy smoothie.
2) Enjoy immediately.

Apple, Spinach & Broccoli Smoothie

Prep time: 10 minutes | Serves: 2 | Per Serving: Calories 136, Carbs 32.9g, Fat 0.6g, Protein 2.6g

Ingredients:

- Large-sized green apple – 1, peeled, cored and cut up
- Broccoli florets – 3-4, cut up
- Fresh spinach – 2 C. Leaves
- Fresh orange juice – 1 C.
- Fresh carrot juice – ½ C.
- Ice cubes – ¼ C.

Directions:

1) Put apple pieces and remnant ingredients into a high-power blender and process to form a smooth and creamy smoothie.
2) Enjoy immediately.

Apple & Green Veggies Smoothie

Prep time: 10 minutes | Serves: 2 | Per Serving: Calories 87, Carbs 21g, Fat 0.6g, Protein 1.5g

Ingredients:

- Green apple, peeled – 1, cored and sliced
- Celery stalk – 1, cut up
- Fresh spinach – 1 C.
- Lettuce – ½ C. cut up
- Fresh Ginger – ¼ tsp. cut up
- Liquid stevia – 3-4 drops
- Fresh lemon juice – ½ tbsp.
- Coconut water – 1 C.
- Ice cubes – ¼ C.

Directions:

1) Put apple and remnant ingredients into a high-power blender and process to form a smooth and creamy smoothie.
2) Enjoy immediately.

Pear & Spinach Smoothie

Prep time: 10 minutes | Serves: 2 | Per Serving: Calories 151, Carbs 37.4g, Fat 0.7g, Protein 2.5g

Ingredients:

- Pears – 2, peeled, cored and sliced
- Fresh spinach – 2 C.
- Liquid stevia – 3-4 drops
- Chilled coconut water – 1 C.
- Chilled filtered water – 1 C.

Directions:

1) Put pears and remnant ingredients into a high-power blender and process to form a smooth and creamy smoothie.
2) Enjoy immediately.

Pear, Grapes & Kale Smoothie

Prep time: 10 minutes | Serves: 2 | Per Serving: Calories 132, Carbs 32.7g, Fat 0.1g, Protein 2.3g

Ingredients:

- Small-sized pear – 1, peeled, cored, and cut up
- Seedless green grapes – 1 C.
- Fresh kale – 2 C. trimmed and cut up
- Fresh lime juice – ½ tbsp.
- Liquid stevia – 3-4 drops
- Fresh lime juice – ½ tbsp.
- Filtered water – 1 C.
- Ice cubes – ¼ C.

Directions:

1) Put pear and remnant ingredients into a high-power blender and process to form a smooth and creamy smoothie.
2) Enjoy immediately.

Pear & Cucumber Smoothie

Prep time: 10 minutes | Serves: 2 | Per Serving: Calories 94, Carbs 23.5g,
Fat 0.6g, Protein 2.1g

Ingredients:

- Small-sized pear – 1, peeled, cored and sliced
- Small-sized cucumber – 1, peeled and cut up
- Fresh dandelion greens – 1 C. cut up
- Liquid stevia – 3-4 drops
- Fresh lemon juice – ½ tbsp.
- Chilled filtered water – 1 C.

Directions:

1) Put pear and remnant ingredients into a high-power blender and process to form a smooth and creamy smoothie.
2) Enjoy immediately.

Kiwi & Avocado Smoothie

Prep time: 10 minutes |Serves: 2 | Per Serving: Calories 185, Carbs 20.3g,
Fat 11.4g, Protein 4.2g

Ingredients:

- Kiwi – 1, peeled and cut up
- Small-sized avocado – 1, peeled, pitted and cut up
- Cucumber – 1 C. peeled and cut up
- Fresh baby kale – 2 C.
- Fresh mint leaves – ¼ C.
- Filtered water – 2 C.
- Ice cubes – ¼ C.

Directions:

1) Put kiwi and remnant ingredients into a high-power blender and process to form a smooth and creamy smoothie.
2) Enjoy immediately.

Cucumber and parsley Smoothie

Prep time: 10 minutes │Serves: 2 │ Per Serving: Calories 40, Carbs 8.1g, Fat 0.6g, Protein 2.5g

Ingredients:

- Cucumber – 2 C. peeled and cut up
- Fresh parsley – 1 C.
- Fresh ginger root 1 (1-inch) piece, peeled and cut up
- Fresh lemon juice – 2 tbsp.
- Liquid stevia – 3-4 drops
- Chilled filtered water – 2 C.

Directions:

1) Put cucumber and remnant ingredients into a high-power blender and process to form a smooth and creamy smoothie.
2) Enjoy immediately.

Zucchini & Spinach Smoothie

Prep time: 10 minutes | Serves: 2 | Per Serving: Calories 117, Carbs 7.5g,
Fat 8.4g, Protein 6.1g

Ingredients:

- Medium-sized zucchini – 1, peeled and cut up roughly
- Fresh spinach – 2 C. cut up
- Peanut butter – 2 tbsp.
- Liquid stevia – 3-4 drops
- Filtered water – 2 C.

Directions:

1) Put zucchini and remnant ingredients into a high-power blender and process to form a smooth and creamy smoothie.
2) Enjoy immediately.

Avocado & Mint Smoothie

Prep time: 10 minutes | Serves: 2 | Per Serving: Calories 149, Carbs 6.6g, Fat 13.7g, Protein 1.8g

Ingredients:

- Small-sized avocado – 1, peeled, pitted and cut up
- Fresh mint leaves – 12-14
- Fresh lime juice – 2 tbsp.
- Vanilla extract – ½ tsp.
- Unsweetened almond milk – 1½ C.
- Ice cubes – ¼ C.

Directions:

1) Put avocado and remnant ingredients into a high-power blender and process to form a smooth and creamy smoothie.
2) Enjoy immediately.

Avocado & Greens Smoothie

Prep time: 10 minutes │Serves: 2 │ Per Serving: Calories 154, Carbs 11.9g,
Fat 11.6g, Protein 3.5g

Ingredients:

- Small-sized avocado – 1, peeled, pitted and cut up
- Fresh spinach – 1¼ C.
- Fresh arugula – 1¼ C.
- Fresh ginger – 1 (1-inch) piece, peeled and cut up
- Fresh parsley – ¾ C,
- Pinch of salt
- Coconut water – 1 C.
- Ice cubes – ½ C.

Directions:

1) Put avocado and remnant ingredients into a high-power blender and process to form a smooth and creamy smoothie.
2) Enjoy immediately.

Protein Spinach Smoothie

Prep time: 10 minutes | Serves: 2 | Per Serving: Calories 208, Carbs 6.7g, Fat 14g, Protein 16.4g

Ingredients:

- Fresh spinach – 2 C.
- Frozen avocado – ½ C.
- Almond butter – 1 tbsp.
- Unsweetened protein powder – 1 scoop
- Liquid stevia – 3-4 drops
- Unsweetened almond milk – 1 C.
- Vanilla extract – 1 tsp.
- Ice cubes – 1 C.

Directions:

1) Put spinach and remnant ingredients into a high-power blender and process to form a smooth and creamy smoothie.
2) Enjoy immediately.

Grapes & Avocado Smoothie

Prep time: 10 minutes | Serves: 2 | Per Serving: Calories 188, Carbs 23.7g,
Fat 11.1g, Protein 1.1g

Ingredients:

- Seedless green grapes – 1¼ C.
- Small-sized avocado – 1, peeled, pitted and cut up
- Liquid stevia – 3-4 drops
- Green tea – 1½ C. brewed and cooled
- Ice cubes – ¼ C.

Directions:

1) Put grapes and remnant ingredients into a high-power blender and process to form a smooth and creamy smoothie.
2) Enjoy immediately.

Grapes & Veggies Smoothie

Prep time: 10 minutes | Serves: 2 | Per Serving: Calories 170, Carbs 29.2g, Fat 3.3g, Protein 6.9g

Ingredients:

- Seedless green grapes – 1 C.
- Broccoli florets – ¼ C. cut up
- Carrot – ¼ C. peeled and cut up
- Fresh spinach – 1 C.
- Unsweetened almond milk – 1½ C.
- Ice cubes – ¼ C.

Directions:

1) Put grapes and remnant ingredients into a high-power blender and process to form a smooth and creamy smoothie.
2) Enjoy immediately.

Grapefruit & Cucumber Smoothie

Prep time: 10 minutes | Serves: 2 | Per Serving: Calories 102, Carbs 18.2g, Fat 0.3g, Protein 6.7g

Ingredients:

- Large-sized Grapefruit – 1, peeled, seeded and sectioned
- Fresh Dandelion Greens – 1 C.
- Small-sized Cucumber – ½, peeled and cut up
- Celery Stalk – 1, cut up
- Fat-free milk – 1¼ C.
- Ice cubes – ¼ C.

Directions:

1) Put grapefruit pieces and remnant ingredients into a high-power blender and process to form a smooth and creamy smoothie.
2) Enjoy immediately.

Green Veggies Smoothie

Prep time: 10 minutes | Serves: 2 | Per Serving: Calories 42, Carbs 8.5g, Fat 0.4g, Protein 2g

Ingredients:

- Fresh spinach – ½ C.
- Fresh kale – ½ C.
- Broccoli florets – ¼ C. cut up
- Green Cabbage – ¼ C. cut up
- Small-sized Green bell pepper – ½, seeded and cut up
- Liquid stevia – 3-4 drops
- Chilled coconut water – 1½ C.

Directions:

1) Put spinach and remnant ingredients into a high-power blender and process to form a smooth and creamy smoothie.
2) Enjoy immediately.

Cucumber and avocado Smoothie

Prep time: 10 minutes | Serves: 2 | Per Serving: Calories 148, Carbs 11.8g, Fat 11.4g, Protein 2.6g

Ingredients:

- Large-sized cucumber – 1, peeled and cut up
- Small-sized avocado – 1, peeled, pitted and cut up
- Fresh Mint Leaves – ¼ C.
- Fresh ginger – ¼ tsp. cut up
- Fresh lemon juice – 2 tbsp.
- Chilled filtered water – 2 C.

Directions:

1) Put cucumber and remnant ingredients into a high-power blender and process to form a smooth and creamy smoothie.
2) Enjoy immediately.

Herbed Green Smoothie

Prep time: 10 minutes | Serves: 2 | Per Serving: Calories 164, Carbs 13.4g, Fat 11.5g, Protein 5.4g

Ingredients:

- Filtered water – 1 C.
- Fat-free Plain Yogurt – ½ C.
- Medium-sized avocado – 1, peeled, pitted and cut up
- Fresh dandelion greens – 1 C.
- Fresh spinach – 1 C. cut up
- Fresh parsley leaves – ¼ C.
- Fresh mint leaves – ¼ C.
- Ice cubes – ¼ C.

Directions:

1) Put avocado and remnant ingredients into a high-power blender and process to form a smooth and creamy smoothie.
2) Enjoy immediately.

Spinach Chia Smoothie

Prep time: 10 minutes | Serves: 2 | Per Serving: Calories 85, Carbs 9g, Fat 5.3g, Protein 4.8g

Ingredients:

- Fresh spinach – 3 C.
- Chia seeds – 2 tbsp.
- Matcha green tea powder – 2 tsp.
- Fresh lemon juice – ½ tsp.
- Xanthan gum – ½ tsp.
- Liquid stevia – 3-4 drops
- Fat-free plain Greek yogurt – 4 tbsp.
- Unsweetened almond milk – 1½ C.
- Ice cubes – ¼ C.

Directions:

1) Put spinach and remnant ingredients into a high-power blender and process to form a smooth and creamy smoothie.
2) Enjoy immediately.

Conclusion

In closing, the world of diabetic-friendly smoothies is an exciting journey filled with flavors, colors, and wholesome ingredients. This recipe book aims to be your trusty guide, offering a rich repertoire of recipes catering to your health needs and taste buds. As you embark on this newfound adventure, remember that these smoothies are not just about managing your blood sugar levels but also about savoring life's sweet moments in a mindful and health-conscious way. Whether you're a seasoned chef or a novice in the kitchen, these recipes are here to inspire your culinary creativity. So, blend and enjoy every sip, knowing you're moving towards a healthier and happier you. May your smoothie-making endeavors be as vibrant as the fruits and as fulfilling as the knowledge that you're nurturing your well-being with each delicious concoction. Cheers to your journey toward a balanced and flavorful life!

give up our favorite meals and flavors to stay on track... if we told you that you don't have to sacrifice taste and well-being? This book is your guide to creating smoothies that not only fit within the bounds of your diabetic diet but also tantalize your taste buds.

Printed in Great Britain
by Amazon

40054126R00034